Buying a condo in the Philippines

Secrets and tips

Arthur Crandon LL.B (Hons), M.A.

The Secrets of Condo Buying in the Philippines

© 2024 by Arthur Crandon

All rights reserved. No part of this book may be reproduced, stored in a retrieval system, or transmitted in any form or by any means—electronic, mechanical, photocopying, recording, or otherwise—without the prior written permission of the publisher, except for brief quotations in critical reviews or articles.

This is a work of fiction. Names, characters, places, and incidents are either the product of the author's imagination or used fictitiously. Any resemblance to actual persons, living or dead, events, or locales is entirely coincidental.

ISBN: 9798334817296

Cover design by Lance Ceniza

Interior design and formatting by Lynnie Ceniza

Published by Arthur Crandon Publishing

Visit our website: Arthurcrandon.co.uk

DISCLAIMER

The information provided in this book is for general informational purposes only. It does not constitute legal, financial, or professional advice. While every effort has been made to ensure accuracy, the author and publisher assume no responsibility for errors or omissions. Readers should consult with appropriate professionals for specific advice tailored to their individual circumstances.

First Edition: July 2024

Visit Arthurcrandon.co.uk for More Titles

CONTENTS

	Acknowledgments	i
1	Advantages of a condo	1
2	Legal steps to buying a condo	9
3	Disadvantages of buying a condo unit	15
4	Where to buy your condo	21

Introduction to Condominium units in the Philippines

Why Condos and not Houses?

Philippines law does not allow foreigners to buy land (Although there are some ways you can do it – see the guide available from our website)

But, foreigners are allowed to buy Condominium Units as they do not sit on land, but rather, are above it. But even so, in any development, foreigners may only own 40 per cent of the units, and filipinos must own 60 per cent of the land the development is built

1 THE ADVANTAGES OF A CONDO

Let's explore the advantages of buying a condo unit in the Philippines. Whether you're an investor, a young professional, or someone seeking a convenient lifestyle, there's something intriguing about those high-rise abodes. Here we go:

1. Market Growth and Stability:

- The Philippine real estate market has been on a steady upward trajectory. Investors can benefit from rental income or property appreciation over time. It's like planting a seed and watching it grow into a sturdy tree—only this tree comes with a view of the city skyline!

- However, be warned, that some developments have been overprice and have taken a long time to sell, and the resell value has been less that the investment.

2. Area Development:

- The archipelago is a mix of bustling metropolises and serene landscapes. Owning a condo in a developing area can be a smart move. Why? Because as that area flourishes, so does your investment. Think of it as being part of a neighborhood's evolution—a front-row seat to progress!

- If maintaining the value of your property is important to you, you would be wise to stick to developments in the bigger cities – Manila, Cebu etc. Prices are not so volatile and developments are always sought after.

3. Financial Leverage:

- Imagine having a secret financial superhero—let's call it "Condo-Man." Owning a condo provides leverage. It's like lifting a heavier weight at the gym—you can achieve more with less effort. Whether you're a local or a foreign investor, this leverage can help you build wealth and expand your portfolio.

4. Increased Buying Power:

- Picture this: You're at the real estate buffet, and your plate is suddenly bigger. That's what owning a condo does—it boosts your overall buying power. Banks and loan companies nod approvingly when you own property. Suddenly, that dream of owning a beachfront villa seems a bit more attainable!

5. Additional Income Sources:

- Condos are like Swiss Army knives—they come with extra tools. You can rent out your unit, turning it into a cash flow machine. Or maybe you'll Airbnb it to travelers seeking a cozy nest. Either way, it's like having a side hustle that pays the bills while you sip your morning coffee.

6. Passive Income:

- Ah, the sweet sound of money rolling in without much effort. Owning a condo can provide passive income. Just imagine: You're sipping piña coladas on a beach, and your condo is busy earning rent. It's like having a well-behaved pet that doesn't shed—pure bliss! 🌴

Remember, condos often come with amenities—swimming pools, gyms, and maybe even a rooftop garden where you can practice your yoga poses. Plus, they're usually situated near central business districts, making that daily commute a breeze.

2 LEGAL STEPS TO BUYING A CONDO

Buying a condominium in the Philippines involves several legal steps to ensure a smooth and secure transaction. Here's a detailed guide to help you navigate the process:

1. **Research and Property Hunting**

- **Identify Your Needs**: Determine your budget, preferred location, and the type of condominium you want.

- **Find a Reputable Developer**: Look for developers with a good track record to avoid potential issues.

2. **Check Legal Requirements**

- **Foreign Ownership**: Foreigners can own condominium units in the Philippines as long as no more than 40% of the units in a single project are owned by foreigners[1].

- **Eligibility**: Ensure you meet the legal requirements, such as being at least 21 years old and having a valid passport[2].

3. Secure Financing

- **Payment Options**: Decide whether you will pay in cash or through a loan. If opting for a loan, get pre-approved by a bank or financing institution[3].

4. Make an Offer

- **Reservation Agreement**: Once you find a suitable unit, sign a reservation agreement and pay the reservation fee to hold the unit[4].

- **Contract to Sell**: Review and sign the Contract to Sell, which outlines the terms and conditions of the sale[4].

5. Prepare Required Documents

- **Identification**: Provide government-issued IDs, proof of income, and a tax identification number[3].

- **Additional Documents**: Depending on the developer or financing institution, you may need to submit additional documents[3].

6. Legal Review

- **Hire a Lawyer**: It's advisable to hire a lawyer to review all documents and ensure everything is in order[3].

- **Due Diligence**: Conduct due diligence to verify the legitimacy of the property and the developer[5].

7. Closing the Deal

- **Deed of Absolute Sale**: Once all conditions are met, sign the Deed of Absolute Sale, which transfers ownership from the seller to the buyer[4].

- **Payment**: Complete the payment as per the agreed terms.

8. Transfer of Title

- **Register the Title**: Submit the Deed of Absolute Sale to the Registry of Deeds to have the title transferred to your name[4].

- **Pay Taxes and Fees**: Pay the necessary taxes and fees, including documentary stamp tax, transfer tax, and registration fees[4].

9. Turnover and Move-In

- **Inspection**: Inspect the unit to ensure it meets the agreed specifications before taking possession[1].

- **Certificate of Title**: Receive the Certificate of Title and other relevant documents from the developer[1].

10. Post-Purchase Responsibilities

- **Condo Dues**: Be aware of monthly condo dues and other fees associated with owning a condominium[4].

- **Property Management**: Understand the rules and regulations of the condominium corporation[6].

By following these steps, you can ensure a smooth and legally compliant process when buying a condominium in the Philippines. Always seek professional advice to navigate the complexities of real estate transactions.

3 DISADVANTAGES OF BUYING A CONDO UNIT

Buying a condominium in the Philippines can be an attractive option, but it's important to be aware of the potential disadvantages. Here are some key points to consider:

1. Limited Space

- **Smaller Living Area**: Condos typically offer less space compared to houses, which can be a drawback if you need more room for your belongings or prefer a larger living area[1].

- **Shared Walls**: Living in close proximity to neighbors can lead to noise and privacy concerns[2].

2. Monthly Fees

- **Condo Dues**: Owners are required to pay monthly condominium fees for the maintenance of common areas and amenities. These fees can add up over time and may increase periodically[2].

- **Special Assessments**: Occasionally, condo associations may levy special assessments for major repairs or improvements, which can be an unexpected expense[3].

3. Limited Control

- **Management Decisions**: As a condo owner, you have limited control over the management and maintenance of the building. Decisions are typically made by the condo association, which may not always align with your preferences[2].

- **Rules and Regulations**: Condos often have strict rules and regulations that residents must follow, which can limit your freedom to make changes to your unit or use common areas[2].

4. Potential for Declining Value

- **Market Volatility**: The value of condo units can be more volatile compared to single-family homes. Factors such as overdevelopment in the area or changes in the local real estate market can affect property values[1].

- **Building Age**: As buildings age, they may require more maintenance and repairs, which can impact the resale value of your unit[3].

- Another consideration if you are buying a new unit, may be that you are not allowed to resell it for a certain number of years. The developers sometimes do this so that resale properties do not come onto the market in competition with the new units they are selling.

5. Hidden Costs

- **Taxes and Fees**: In addition to monthly condo dues, there are other costs such as property taxes, insurance, and utility fees that need to be considered[3].

- **Maintenance Costs**: While condo fees cover common area maintenance, you are still responsible for the upkeep of your own unit, which can include repairs and renovations[3].

6. Resale Challenges

- **Market Competition**: Selling a condo can be challenging, especially in a saturated market where many similar units are available[1].

- **Buyer Preferences**: Some buyers may prefer single-family homes over condos, which can limit your potential market when it comes time to sell[1].

7. Potential for Disputes

- **Neighbor Conflicts**: Living in close quarters with others can sometimes lead to disputes over noise, pets, or use of common areas[2].

- **Condo Association Issues**: Disagreements over management decisions or rule enforcement can also arise[2].

Considering these disadvantages can help you make an informed decision about whether buying a condo is the right choice for you. It's always a good idea to weigh the pros and cons and consult with a real estate professional before making a purchase.

4 WHERE IS THE BEST PLACE TO BUY A CONDO

Choosing the best place to buy a condo in the Philippines depends on various factors such as lifestyle preferences, budget, and long-term goals. Here are some of the top locations to consider, each with its unique advantages:

1. Metro Manila

- **Makati**: Known as the financial hub of the Philippines, Makati offers a vibrant urban lifestyle with numerous shopping centers, restaurants, and entertainment options. It's ideal for those who want to be in the heart of the action and enjoy a cosmopolitan lifestyle[1].

- **Bonifacio Global City (BGC)**: BGC is a modern, upscale area with high-end condos, international schools, and corporate offices. It's perfect for professionals and families looking for a safe and well-planned community[1].

- **Quezon City**: This area offers a mix of residential and commercial spaces, with more affordable condo options compared to Makati and BGC. It's a great choice for those looking for a balance between urban living and budget-friendly options[1].

2. Cebu City

- **Central Visayas**: Cebu City is a major economic and cultural center in the Visayas region. It offers a mix of urban and beach lifestyles, with numerous condo developments catering to different budgets. The city is known for its historical sites, vibrant nightlife, and proximity to beautiful beaches[2].

3. Davao City

- **Mindanao**: Davao City is known for its safety, cleanliness, and low cost of living. It's an excellent choice for retirees and families looking for a peaceful environment. The city also offers beautiful natural attractions like Mount Apo and Samal Island[3].

4. Subic Bay

- **Central Luzon**: Subic Bay is a former U.S. naval base that has been transformed into a thriving commercial and residential area. It offers a secure environment, modern amenities, and beautiful coastal views. It's ideal for those seeking a quieter lifestyle with easy access to outdoor activities[4].

5. Tagaytay

- **Cavite**: Known for its cool climate and scenic views of Taal Volcano, Tagaytay is a popular weekend getaway spot. It's also becoming a favored location for condo buyers who want a serene environment while still being relatively close to Metro Manila[5].

6. Iloilo City

- **Western Visayas**: Iloilo City is known for its rich cultural heritage, friendly locals, and growing economy. The city offers a mix of modern and traditional living, with new condo developments catering to various lifestyles[2].
-

Factors to Consider

- **Budget**: Determine your budget and

look for areas that offer condos within your price range.
- **Lifestyle**: Consider your lifestyle preferences, such as proximity to work, schools, shopping centers, and recreational activities.
- **Future Development**: Look for areas with upcoming infrastructure projects and developments, as these can increase property values over time.
- **Safety and Security**: Ensure the area has a good reputation for safety and security.

Each of these locations has its unique charm and advantages, so it's essential to visit and explore them to see which one aligns best with your needs and preferences.

We publish an extensive range of books all about the Philippines from a westerners point of view.

Check them out on our website:

ac@arthurcrandon.co.uk

ABOUT THE AUTHOR

Arthur Crandon is a retired lawyer and a prolific writer. Hi is British and grew up in a rural community in Somerset. He has lived in England, Wales, Hong Kong and the Philippines and now spends most of his time in the Philippines with his Visayan wife and their son.

He loves to hear from anyone who has anything to do with the Philippines – you can email him anytime on:

ac@arthurcrandon.co.uk

www.ingramcontent.com/pod-product-compliance
Lightning Source LLC
Chambersburg PA
CBHW072049230526
45479CB00009B/328